AF606917

INVESTIGATING GHOSTS IN HOSPITALS

Matilda Snowden

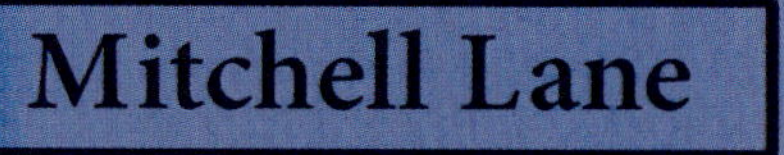

PUBLISHERS

mitchelllane.com

2001 SW 31st Avenue
Hallandale, FL 33009

First Edition, 2021.
Author: Matilda Snowden
Designer: Ed Morgan
Editor: Joyce Markovics

Series: Investigating Ghosts!
Title: Investigating Ghosts in Hospitals / by Matilda Snowden

Hallandale, FL : Mitchell Lane Publishers, [2021]

Library bound ISBN: 978-1-68020-631-9
eBook ISBN: 978-1-68020-632-6

PHOTO CREDITS: Design Elements, freepik.com, p. 5 Shutterstock.com, p. 7 Nathan Wright on Unsplash, p. 9 Royasfoto73 CC-BY-SA-4.0, p. 13 Photo by Andrew Amistad on Unsplash, p, 15 loc.gov, p. 16-19 Richie Diesterheft CC-BY-2.0, p. 17 Pauselife71 CC-BY-SA-4.0, p. 18 Vidar Nordli-Mathisen on Unsplash, p. 21 Crash575 CC-BY-SA-3.0, p. 23 Pauselife71 CC-BY-SA-4.0, p. 25 Nicolas Henderson CC BY 2.0

Contents

Words in **bold** can be found in the Glossary.

CHAPTER ONE

HAUNTED HOSPITALS

Nestled on a hill is an abandoned hospital. Lining the front of the building are broken windows resembling dark, hollow eyes. A ghost hunter enters through the front door, stepping over shards of glass. As he makes his way into a small, white room, tingles shoot up his spine. "Is there anyone present?" he asks, clutching an audio recorder. He listens carefully. No response.

Then he asks the question again. A deep voice whispers, "Help me!" The ghost hunter whips around. *Creak, creak. Creak, creak.* A door on the other side of the room swings open. But no one is there.

Hospitals are places where sick people go to get better. However, in the past, hospitals were often where people went to die. Many were overcrowded, dirty, and the treatments did more harm than good. Is this why so many old hospitals are said to be haunted? Do the **spirits** of the dead linger in places of suffering? And what spooky secrets are hidden in the walls of these hospitals? There is a **devoted** group of people who want to find out. These ghost hunters, also known as **paranormal** investigators, gather **evidence** to prove that ghosts are real.

Turn the page to read blood-curdling stories about reportedly haunted hospitals and other **institutions**. And follow teams of paranormal investigators who seek to uncover the truth about ghosts.

INTERESTING FACT

Special hospitals called sanatoriums and asylums were once very common. Sanatoriums are where people with chronic diseases went for treatment. Mentally ill people were often treated in asylums.

WAVERLY HILLS SANATORIUM

Louisville, Kentucky

At the Waverly Hills Sanatorium, some patients checked in and never checked out. In the early 1900s, there was an outbreak of tuberculosis (TB), a deadly lung disease. Doctors sent people with TB to Waverly Hills for treatment. However, even with the best care, patients died on an almost daily basis. Their spirits are said to remain in the building where they breathed their last breath. It's no wonder ghost hunters are drawn there.

Waverly Hills is said to have many paranormal hotspots, including the fourth floor and "body chute." This 500-foot long tunnel was used to secretly move dead bodies from inside the **morgue** outside the hospital. In 2001, Keith Age of the Louisville Ghost Hunters Society went to the building in search of ghosts. What he found was shocking.

INTERESTING FACT

In the 1900s, over 100,000 Americans died from TB each year. The highly **contagious** disease was known as "The White **Plague**." Why? Sufferers often grew very weak and pale before they died.

Keith and his team started in the morgue. They brought ghost-hunting tools, including various cameras and an EMF (**electromagnetic field**) meter, which can detect changes in energy fields. Some people believe that ghosts are a form of energy, and when they appear, they can disrupt energy fields. Immediately, Keith's EMF meter went off. And it detected something moving.

"As I got to the center of the room, the meter spiked . . . and squealed to a pitch that I had never heard it make before," said Keith. Then the EMF meter started heating up in his hand—and part of it melted! Just then, the room suddenly grew colder, dropping from 74 to 52 degrees Fahrenheit. Keith could find no explanation for the broken meter or drastic temperature change.

INTERESTING FACT

Keith later learned that the room where his meter spiked was where some TB patients got electroshock therapy. Later, when he was looking at the photos taken by his crew, he saw what appeared to be a light bulb. Yet there were no lights in the building at the time. "I simply couldn't explain what turned out in the photograph," Keith said.

Another day, ghost hunter and author Troy Taylor joined Keith at Waverly Hills. They went to a room on the fourth floor with an EMF meter and video camera. Right away, the meter began picking up activity. Out of nowhere, Troy saw an empty soda bottle fly across the room. It hit Keith in the back. *Boom!* Then a light fixture crashed down from the ceiling, smacking Keith on the head. Finally, a brick slid on its own across the floor. It flew up and whacked Keith in the lower back. It was one of "the most chilling events" Troy had ever seen.

During another visit to the fourth floor, Troy saw "the clear and distinct **silhouette** of a man" in a hallway. Then it **vanished**. "The sighting only lasted a few seconds, but I knew what I had seen," said Troy. "I can count the times I have seen ghosts on just two fingers and one of them was at Waverly Hills."

INTERESTING FACT

Waverly Hills Sanatorium opened in 1926 and closed in 1961. The building was then used as a nursing home for 20 years. Today, the new owners of the sanatorium offer year-round ghost tours.

Trans-Allegheny Lunatic Asylum

Weston, West Virginia

"I don't want to believe in ghosts or the **supernatural**, but I've seen things that are hard to explain in any other way," said Rebecca Jordan Gleason. Rebecca is the building manager at the Trans-Allegheny Lunatic Asylum. The huge, stone building was constructed between 1858 and 1881 on a large piece of land. At that time, it was believed that fresh air and open spaces helped people recover from illness.

In 1864, the hospital opened its doors. It was soon filled to capacity with 250 patients. Over the years, more than 2,400 people—from drug addicts to sick children—were crammed into Trans-Allegheny. The result was overcrowding, unsafe conditions, cruel treatments, and many deaths.

INTERESTING FACT

In 1994, Trans-Allegheny closed its doors for good. Many of the patients who died there are buried in unmarked graves on hospital grounds.

Some mentally ill patients were locked in cages. Others were dunked in freezing cold water or underwent electroshock therapy. Still others were forced to have a **lobotomy**. Sometimes, very sick patients attacked each other or the staff. One day, a nurse was found dead at the bottom of a staircase. Had a patient pushed her? It's thought that hundreds, or perhaps thousands, of people suffered and died at the hospital.

Today, visitors to the Trans-Allegheny Lunatic Asylum have had many ghostly encounters. Rebecca, the building manager, had her own spooky experience. She saw 40 doors open in a hallway and then slam all at once. *Bang!* "One would be pretty scary," she said. "Forty at once was terrifying."

An Automated Data Acquisition Module created by Ghost hunter Michael Baker of Para-Boston helps find ghosts.

INTERESTING FACT

Ghost hunters use lots of equipment to perform their work, such as video cameras, audio recorders, thermal imaging tools to capture hot or cold spots, and special meters that pick up energy fields. They collect evidence to either prove or disprove the existence of ghosts.

Other people have heard **disembodied** voices, loud banging, and ghostly **gurneys** rolling in hallways. They've also felt unexplained cold spots and seen shadows that look like people. During an investigation, Grant Wilson of the Atlantic Paranormal Society saw a full-body **apparition** of a boy. At first, the boy stood motionless in the corner of a room. Then, he raised his arms and looked like he was "being sucked out of the room" by an unseen force, Grant remembers. Grant had never seen anything like it. Are these and other eyewitness accounts proof that Trans-Allegheny is haunted?

MEDICAL CENTER

CHAPTER FOUR

METROPOLITAN STATE HOSPITAL

Waltham, Massachusetts

In 2011, the police received a call that a woman was **trespassing** near the abandoned Metropolitan State Hospital. This was no ordinary woman, however. The 15 witnesses who saw her said she was "glowing blue." When the police arrived, they found no such blue ghost. But the witnesses were sure of what they had seen. Many people, including local ghost hunters, think the blue ghost could be the spirit of Anne Marie Davee.

Anne was a patient at the hospital who disappeared in 1978. Two months later, hospital staff found bits of her clothing on a male patient. Workers also found a **hatchet**. They later discovered seven of Anne's teeth with the man. After an investigation, police discovered that the man had killed Anne and chopped up her body with the hatchet. He buried her in three different places around the hospital. One of those places was a small shack.

INTERESTING FACT

The Metropolitan State Hospital was open from 1927 to 1992. Over 300 patients who died there are buried at nearby Metfern Cemetery.

Paranormal investigator Laura Giuliano was walking around the property one day when she experienced an "**ominous** feeling." Suddenly, she stumbled upon the ruins of a shack. Then she spotted a woman's leather shoe and an old bed sheet. "My heart jumped," Laura said. Did the items belong to Anne Marie Davee? "I wondered if I had uncovered the exact spot where a brutal murder had taken place," said Laura.

Laura also recorded the sound of singing children in the empty hospital. What could explain this? In 2013, investigators from Paranormal New England went to Metropolitan State Hospital. They sat quietly for over an hour with a very sensitive microphone. "What was the most eerie was the sound of children singing," said one investigator. They also felt a sudden temperature drop. They later learned that several children died at the hospital when doctors who were trying to help them accidentally poisoned them.

INTERESTING FACT

Ghost hunter Michael Baker of Para-Boston says, "I can say confidently from what I've found that paranormal phenomenon is real." He also says that it can take weeks, or even years, to find evidence.

YORKTOWN MEMORIAL HOSPITAL

Yorktown, Texas

Ghost hunter Jamie Davis immediately felt uncomfortable when she arrived at Yorktown Memorial Hospital. "The place is straight out of a horror movie," she said. She had also heard stories about **phantom** voices and organ music in the abandoned hospital. Most startling of all were the reports of unseen hands scratching and choking people. Jamie also heard a disturbing story from Mike, the hospital's caretaker. One night, he was walking in a dark hallway with his

girlfriend when he saw something crawling quickly along the floor. At first, he thought it was his dog that had gotten loose. As the thing got closer, he saw that it had the **distorted** face of a woman. Mike said he will "never forget her face."

INTERESTING FACT

Yorktown Memorial Hospital opened in 1951 and was run by nuns. It closed in 1986. An estimated 2,000 people died there.

Jamie and her ghost-hunting partner Sam began their investigation in the hospital's basement. They used flashlights, an audio recorder, and an EMF meter. Suddenly, the meter lit up. "From that point forward, I felt as though someone was following me," Jamie said. Sam immediately began recording. He recorded an unknown female saying "Jamie" over and over again. Then Jamie felt someone breathing on her. Later, she asked the spirit to turn on one of the flashlights, which it did. Jamie had such an uneasy feeling that she left the hospital right away. After the investigation, she said, "This is the scariest place I've ever been." Is it also one of the most haunted?

Ghost-Hunting Tools

Here are some basic ghost-hunting tools. Many household items can be used to track and gather evidence of possible ghosts.

- Pen and paper to record your findings
- A flashlight with extra batteries
- A camera with a clean lens. Sometimes, the "**orbs**" that some people capture on film are actually dust particles on the lens.
- A cell phone to use in case of an emergency and to keep track of time
- A camcorder or digital video recorder to capture images of spirits or any other paranormal activity
- A digital audio recorder to capture ghostly sounds or EVPs
- A digital thermometer to pick up temperature changes

More experienced ghost hunters use thermal imaging tools to locate hot and cold spots, as well as special meters to pick up energy fields. These include EMF (electromagnetic field) and RF (radio frequency) meters.

Find Out More

BOOKS

Gardner Walsh, Liza. *Ghost Hunter's Handbook: Supernatural Explorations for Kids*. Lanham, Maryland: Down East Publishing, 2016.

Loh-Hagan, Virginia. *Odd Jobs: Ghost Hunter*. Ann Arbor, Michigan: Cherry Lake Publishing, 2016.

Williams, Dinah. *Abandoned Insane Asylums*. New York: Bearport Publishing, 2008.

WEBSITES

American Hauntings
https://www.americanhauntingsink.com

American Paranormal Investigations
https://www.ap-investigations.com

American Paranormal Research Association
https://www.apraparanormal.com

American Society for Psychical Research, Inc.
http://www.aspr.com

The Atlantic Paranormal Society
http://the-atlantic-paranormal-society.com

Ghost Research Society
http://www.ghostresearch.org

The Parapsychological Association
https://www.parapsych.org

Works Consulted

Davis, Jamie. *Haunted Asylums, Prisons, and Sanatoriums*. Woodbury, Minnesota: Llewellyn Publications, 2013.

Estep, Richard. *Visiting the Ghost Ward: Inside the World's Most Haunted Hospitals and Asylums*. New York: Rosen, 2017.

Estep, Richard. T*he World's Most Haunted Hospitals: True-Life Paranormal Encounters in Asylums, Hospitals, and Institutions*. Wayne, New Jersey: The Career Press, 2016.

Knowles, Zachery. T*rue Ghost Stories: Real Haunted Hospitals and Mental Asylums*. Scotts Valley, California: CreateSpace, 2015.

Newman, Rich. *Ghost Hunting for Beginners: Everything You Need to Know to Get Started*. Woodbury, Minnesota: Llewellyn Publications, 2018.

Taylor, Troy. *The Ghost Hunters Guidebook: The Essential Guide to Investigating Ghosts & Hauntings*. Alton, Illinois: Whitechapel Productions Press, 2004.

On the Internet

https://www.ksat.com/halloween/haunting/is-abandoned-south-texas-hospital-really-empty

http://www.louisvilleghs.com/LGHS_MASTER/SUB/Investigations/Waverly/Waverly_Hills_Sanatorium.html

https://www.metro.us/boston/for-para-boston-ghost-hunting-is-a-science-not-an-art/zsJnjC---5ydKL7kvzHYRw

http://national-paranormal-society.org/yorktown-memorial-hospital/

http://paranormalnewengland.com/metropolitan-state-hospital/

http://trans-alleghenylunaticasylum.com/main/history.html

GLOSSARY

apparition
A ghost or ghostlike image

chronic
Persisting for a long time

contagious
Easily spread from one person to another; usually a disease

devoted
Very loyal

disembodied
Separated from or existing without a body

distorted
Twisted out of shape

electromagnetic field
A field of energy around a magnetic material or a moving electric charge

electroshock therapy
A medical treatment that uses electricity to shock the brain

evidence
Information and facts that help prove something

gurneys
A wheeled stretcher for transporting patients

hatchet
A small ax

institution
An organization providing care for people with special needs

lobotomy
A surgery in which a patient's brain is cut; formerly used to treat mental illness

morgue
A place where dead bodies are kept

ominous
Giving the feeling that something bad is going to happen

orbs
Glowing spheres

paranormal
Events not able to be scientifically explained

phantom
Belonging to a ghost or spirit

phenomenon
An occurrence that one can sense

plague
A disease that spreads quickly and often kills many people

silhouette
The dark shape and outline of someone or something

spirits
Supernatural beings such as ghosts

supernatural
Beyond scientific understanding

thermal
Relating to heat

trespassing
Entering a place without permission

vanished
Disappeared

INDEX

ABOUT THE AUTHOR

Matilda Snowden loves visiting abandoned buildings and all things old and cobwebby. Her favorite thing about being an author is talking with children about how to tell a spooky story.